Going Deep Point

CRAFTING UNPUTDOWNABLE FICTION

BETH YARNALL

www.BethYarnall.com

Going Deep Into Deep Point of View
Beth Yarnall

Copyright © 2016 by Elizabeth A. Yarnall

All rights reserved under the Pan-American and International Copyright Conventions.

The reproduction, distribution, or transmission of this book in whole or part, by any means, without the express written permission of the author is unlawful piracy and theft of the author's intellectual property.

This book includes sample works of fiction. Names, places, characters, and events are either the product of the author's imagination or are used fictitiously. Any resemblance to actual events, locales, or persons, living or dead, is entirely coincidental.

Any trademarks, service marks, product names, or named features are the property of their respective owners and are used only for reference.

Print ISBN: 978-1940811826
Digital ISBN: 978-1940811888

Editor: Laurie Larsen
Cover Design: Humble Nations

Going Deep Into
Deep Point of View

---•---

CRAFTING UNPUTDOWNABLE FICTION

Table of Contents

Introduction 1
What is Point of View? 5
The Different Types of POV 7
How to Choose the Right Point of View
    for a Scene 19
How to Change Point of View 25
Common Point of View Violations 35
Male vs. Female Point of View 41
What Is Deep Point of View? 45
Using the Five Senses to Achieve Deep POV . 53
Visceral or Physical Reactions in Deep POV .. 61
Internal Dialog and Introspection in
    Deep Point of View 67
Deep Point of View in Dialog 77
Narrowing the Lens 91
In Closing 95
Bibliography 97
About the Author 101

Introduction

Have you ever read a book that grabbed you on the first page and pulled you through the whole book almost nonstop to the end? Did you have a difficult time putting it down? Did you lose sleep, miss your train or bus stop or put off work so you could stay in the world the author created a little bit longer? Have you ever been sad at the thought of never getting to spend time with those characters ever again when the book ended? Was your sadness lifted by the knowledge that there were more books in the series and you happily bought them all?

    If you answered *yes* to all or most of the above questions then the author did his or her job. How did he do it? He used deep point of view. The author not only created interesting characters, he gave them the camera and allowed you, the reader, to experience the events in the book through the point of view characters' eyes. You cried when they cried. You laughed when they laughed. You were worried when they were in peril. For a time you lived as those characters, not only inhabiting their world but the very skin they wore.

In this book we'll take a look at how the author achieved deep point of view (POV). We'll discuss the different kinds of POV, how to choose which character's POV to be in, and how to change POV. We'll take a look at how word choice can draw your reader deeper into your characters' POV, including avoiding filtering words, using the five senses, and visceral or physical reactions. We'll learn the difference between a reliable narrator and an unreliable narrator and how to use each technique effectively. We'll talk about using subtext and internal thoughts to give the reader insight that the characters themselves may not have. And we'll go over which kinds of point of view are commonly used in which genres.

There's a lot to learn, but by reading the examples presented and by completing the exercises in this book you should walk away with some solid practical knowledge about deep point of view that you can use in your own work in whichever genre you write.

Author's Note

In this book I've presented samples from other authors' work (with proper credit) as well as my own. Not because I think my writing is special or precious, but because sometimes it was the most expedient way for me to illustrate a particular point. I could talk all day long about how to do something, but sometimes that's not enough. You have to see the principle in action in order to fully take it in.

I hope you enjoy these authors' excerpts as much as I do and will consider reading one or more of their books. Many are award-winning and best-selling authors. I promise you won't be disappointed.

What Is Point of View?

Point of view is the lens through which the reader *sees* the story. Imagine a camera attached to the top of your character's head. The camera can only capture what your point of view character experiences. It can't know what the other characters in the story think or feel. Nor can it see what the other characters see. It's a single perspective much like in real life.

No matter which point of view you choose for your novel, you're going to be limited to that character's experiences, memories, knowledge, sensation, and emotions. You can only show your reader what the POV character sees, hears, witnesses, is told about, thinks about, and feels. In real life we can guess at what others might be thinking or feeling, but we don't know—we can't *know*—unless we're told. It's the same with our characters. Characters can guess—either correctly or incorrectly—at another character's mindset or emotions based on clues he gets from facial expressions, body language, and tone of voice.

Imagine you're in a meeting in a conference room with twelve other people.

Physically each person in the room has only one vantage point from which they can view the room. The woman standing at the front of the room giving the presentation has the advantage of being able to see the faces of everyone at the table. The man at the back of the room has a view of the backs of everyone's heads—only the woman giving the presentation can see his face. The people in the middle have a view of the people in front of them, but not those sitting behind them. Each attendee *sees* something different.

Everyone in the room is given the same presentation yet each individual will take away something different from the meeting. Why is that? It's because every person attending the meeting brought their own unique experiences, prejudices, emotions, and goals for what they want to learn into the room with them. They're filtering everything through their emotions, experiences, prejudices, preconceived notions, and mindsets.

This is your camera lens or your character's point of view. It will be unique to the individual in the room just as it will be unique to each character in your novel. Use that in your work.

The Different Types of POV

In genre fiction the most often used points of view are first person, third person, and, to a limited extent, omniscient point of view. Before beginning your novel, you will want to decide which point of view you're going to use. Genre will play an important part in this decision. Be sure to research your genre to find out what the norm is. Thrillers aren't often written in a single first person POV just as cozy mysteries don't often have multiple third person points of view.

Can you write outside the norm? Of course and many have done so successfully. Be aware though that you might be setting yourself up for a harder road than if you'd chosen the accepted point of view for your genre. There will always be mavericks who break the rules spectacularly, but I guarantee they spent time mastering the rules before they broke them. Your goal is to write the best book you can, not reinvent the wheel. Sometimes you can be too clever trying to stand out. So clever that your novel is unreadable and therefore unpublishable. So be careful. Make wise authorial choices and then give your work everything you've got.

Let's go over the different types of point of view.

Omniscient Point of View

Omniscient point of view or a 'God's eye view' is a panoramic view of the whole novel. An unseen narrator relays what is happening. This POV knows all, sees all, and tells all. Notice I said *tells* not *shows*. (We'll talk about *show vs. tell* later in the book.) The unseen narrator is *not* a character in the story. This narrator tells the story from an all-knowing viewpoint. He doesn't enter the heads of the other characters so he can't tell the reader what they're thinking and feeling. He can only relay what they're *doing*. The unseen narrator may even give the reader details of the story that the other characters don't know and may never know.

The Secret Garden by Frances Hodgson Burnette employs omniscient point of view in the very first pages of the book. Epic novels with a large cast of characters such as J.R.R. Tolkien's ***Lord of the Rings*** use omniscient point of view to help manage the sheer volume of characters in the novel. Can you imagine, if he'd spent pages in each character's POV, how huge the books would've been?

Television programs such as the ***Dukes of Hazard*** and ***Desperate Housewives*** used an omniscient narrator to great effect by creating tension and expectation when the unseen narrator gives the viewers information that the characters don't have. Think of omniscient point of view like a security camera mounted above your characters' heads rather than a camera mounted to the top of your characters' heads.

An example of omniscient POV from ***The Secret Garden*** by Frances Hodgson Burnette:

When Mary Lennox was sent to Misselwaite Manor to live with her uncle everybody said she was the most disagreeable-looking child ever seen. It was true, too. She had a little thin face and a little thin body, thin light hair and a sour expression. Her hair was yellow and her face was yellow because she'd been born in India and had always been ill in one way or another. Her father had held a position in the English Government and had always been busy and ill himself, and her mother had been a great beauty who cared to only go to parties and amuse herself with gay people.

The narrator is outside the story and the characters, telling the reader information about all of the characters at once.

First Person Point of View

In first person point of view the story is told from the viewpoint of *one* protagonist, usually the main or central character in the book, using pronouns such as I, me, we, us, my, mine, ours. First person point of view gives the reader a sense of immediacy and connects them intimately with the POV character. In this singular viewpoint only what the POV character experiences, sees, feels, hears, or thinks can be relayed to the reader.

Most authors think that writing first person point of view is an automatic ticket to deep point of view. It's not. As with any point of view you choose to write in, you have to watch out for *telling* or *shallow* writing. Because first person can feel like writing a journal, authors can get lazy by using phrases such as *If I'd only known...* or *Looking back I should've realized...* Also the overuse of the pronoun *I* can pull the reader away from your character. If you do a search of your manuscript and you discover

THE DIFFERENT TYPES OF POV

you've started the majority of your sentences with *I*, then you're probably *telling* and not *showing*. Try to rewrite as many of those sentences as you can to deepen the point of view.

You have to have a dynamic, interesting character if you're writing in first person POV. After all, your reader is going to be in the head and heart of this character throughout the entire book. If your character isn't compelling or worst yet, is unlikable, then your reader isn't going to stick around for the end of the book.

An example of first person POV from ***Reclaim*** by Beth Yarnall:

I joke a lot about having bad luck and being cursed. That's not what it is. I'm just one of those people who have to work harder than anyone else. Nothing comes easy to me. I get what I'm after... eventually. Usually on the third or fourth try. Never the first. I envy people who coast through life thinking about wanting something and then bam. *They have it.*

Notice the use of *I* and *me*—the tale-tell sign of first person POV.

Second Person Point of View

The least often used point of view choice in genre fiction is second person point of view. And for good reason. It feels very finger-pointy and intrusive to the reader.

You're late. Heart pounding, you race up the stairs as the train enters the station. You weave around the slow-moving people milling on the platform and dash towards the train, throwing your body through the doorway with only a moment to spare.

See what I mean? Writing in second person POV can make your novel read like a manual or how-to book (like this one!). Not very fun in genre fiction. Second person POV is written using the pronouns you, your, and yours. Occasionally authors writing in other points of view can slip into second POV without realizing it, especially in books with a conversational tone to them like first person POV.

An example would be phrasing such as: *How do you know when you're in love?*

Take a hard look at your usage of *you* in sentences and try to look for a way to rewrite them. You don't want your readers stumbling over your passages trying to decipher which character is speaking.

A good rewrite would be: *Could this feeling be love?*

This rewritten sentence draws the reader in much more than the first. Second person point of view is used most often in nonfiction instructional books and step-by-step guides. It's rarely, if ever used in genre fiction.

Third Person Point of View

The most common used point of view for genre fiction is third person POV. He, she, him, her, his, hers, they, them, their, theirs, it or its are the pronouns used in third person. Typically, when third person is employed, it's used for more than one character such as the protagonist and the antagonist or the hero and heroine.

Here's an example of third person POV from ***A Deep and Dark December*** by Beth Yarnall:

There weren't a great many things that bothered Erin December. For the most part, she considered herself a pretty even-keeled person. So why was her face hot and the back of her throat aching with the words she couldn't let loose? As she sat in the Kavender Investments staff meeting, listening to Ramie Kavender heap praise on Austin for the success of the Petrie project, she couldn't believe what she was hearing.

The character's name is used—Erin December—and the pronoun *she*. Both are characteristic of third person POV.

Multiple Points of View

Depending on the genre you write and what your vision for your story is you can use more than one character's point of view. At all times, no matter which point of view you choose, you will want to make it clear to the reader whose head they're in.

Multiple Third Person Point of View

Most genre fiction employs more than one third person point of view. Typically the point of view of the protagonist and the antagonist or the hero and heroine, but some authors also go into the point of view of a villain or secondary character to reveal something to the reader that the main characters can't. There's no set limit to how many points of view you can use in your novel. Be careful though. Don't bog down your story with unimportant viewpoints and details from periphery characters. Choose your point of view characters wisely and with purpose.

Multiple First Person Point of View

Some authors who write in first person like to explore the point of view of more than one of their characters. As with multiple third person point of views, multiple first person POV can give the reader more information about your story and characters. I suggest limiting first person POV to no more than two characters. The immediacy of first person can wear thin in multiple viewpoints in a way that it doesn't in third person.

Mixed Point of View

Some authors mix point of views, using first person point of view for one character and third person point of view for another. Mixing POVs isn't used often in genre fiction, but that doesn't mean you can't use it if your story calls for this technique. You may come across editors and readers who don't care for mixed POV so be prepared for that feedback.

Whether you write in first person, third person, omniscient or a combination of POVs, the reader should be clear about whose head they're in.

Which POV Is Acceptable in Which Genres?

Before deciding on which point of view to use in your novel it's important to know what POV is acceptable in your genre. Below is a loose guide to the most common type or types of point of view used in genre fiction.

Horror- First person point of view works well in horror as long as your POV character doesn't die. Third person POV is also acceptable.

Fantasy- First or third person point of view, depending on how epic (the number of POV characters—think George R.R. Martin's **Game of Thrones**) your story is.

Mystery/Thriller- Typically mysteries and thrillers will be in third person with two or more points of view. An exception is cozy mysteries, which are almost always first person POV.

Romance- The type of point of view you use in romance will depend on the subgenre.

Contemporary- Third person.

Historical Romance- Third person.

New Adult- First person singular or first person dual point of view.

Paranormal- Either first person or third person.

Suspense- Third person.

SciFi- First person POV or two or more third person points of view.

Women's Fiction- Third person with two or more points of view.

Young Adult- Typically one first person POV. I have seen books that employ more than one first person POV, two or more third person POV or alternating first and third POV. There's a lot of flexibility in YA so use what works best for your story.

I recommend that you read extensively in your genre to learn how other authors use point of view. Find out what works, what doesn't work, and why.

Exercise:

Write a short scene from a different point of view than you normally write. If you typically write in first person try a scene from third and vice versa. What did you learn? Was it easier or harder? Did it make you want to explore writing from a different POV?

How to Choose the Right Point of View for a Scene

Have you ever read a scene in a book that fell flat? Did you stop halfway through and wonder why you were reading it? As an author, have you ever felt that a scene you were writing wasn't working, but you couldn't figure out why?

You were probably writing it from the wrong character's point of view.

If you only have one point of view in your book, then choosing which character's head to be in isn't going to be an issue for you. But if you have more than one POV character then you've got some choices to make. In each scene you're going to have to decide whose head to be in, how long to stay in that point of view, and when to change point of view.

So how do you make those choices?

There are several ways to go about it.

Ask yourself what the scene is supposed to accomplish. How does the scene move the story forward? What new information will be gleaned? Which character's point of view can you use to best accomplish your goals in the scene and deliver that information to the reader? What does the scene reveal about your character's backstory and emotional investment in what is happening in the scene? Use POV to give the reader an intimate glimpse into your character's motivation and how the conflict in the scene might keep her from her goal.

A good rule of thumb is to choose the point of view that's going to give you the most emotional punch, the character who will have the strongest emotional reaction to what is happening in the scene. That might be the character who has the most to lose or the most information to convey. It could be a character who is hiding something he desperately doesn't want the other character/s to know. It could be the character with the most unreasonable or hard to understand response to the scene, the misunderstood character. This might be a character—like the villain—whose beliefs and behavior will be upsetting or confusing to the reader. Unreliable narrators would fall into this last category.

What's an unreliable narrator you ask?

An unreliable narrator is a character whose credibility is seriously compromised. This could be because she refuses to face certain aspects of her character. Something traumatic might have happened to her that she doesn't want to acknowledge or confront. She might be lying to herself about the motivations behind her actions. She might be in denial about her drug or alcohol abuse or previous bad behavior.

In my novel, ***Atone***, the heroine is an unreliable narrator. She comes off as a touch cold and her behavior is difficult to understand at first. As the story progresses the reader learns more about her in bits and pieces. For more emotional impact I chose to be in her point of view when she was forced to reveal and confront the most difficult parts of her past. By the end of the book the reader (hopefully) can't help but cheer for her happily ever after. It wasn't easy keeping so much of her hidden and still keep the reader turning the page.

Tarryn Fisher's ***The Opportunist*** is a great example of an unreliable narrator with questionable motives. We can see the crash and burn coming; it's just a matter of when and how awful it's going to be. Marian Keyes's ***Rachel's Holiday*** is about a character who isn't honest about her problems. She's in such denial she lashes out at the other characters in the book and blames them for the bad things that happen to her and as a reader we do too because we trust her. ***Anybody Out There?*** also by Marian

Keyes features a character who is in deep, deep denial. When the truth about what happened to her is revealed it's a real shocker. That book stayed with me a long time after I read it.

The reader should have some inkling that the point of view character isn't entirely on the up and up, but they may not know to what extent or why the character behaves the way he does until close to the end of the book. The use of the unreliable narrator can be a powerful tool in your author arsenal.

So you've chosen the point of view character for your scene, now what?

Now you write the scene, then take a good hard look at it. Does it work? Are you giving the reader something new? Did it pack enough of an emotional punch? Are your characters better or worse off after the scene is over? I know it's hard, but try to be objective about your work. If you can't, then maybe get a trusted author friend or critic partner to give it a read. If the scene isn't working, if it feels flat or you're not getting the emotion out of it that you want or need...try switching the POV.

Sometimes you have to do it wrong to get it right.

Exercise:

Write a short scene from one character's point of view (either first or third person). Then rewrite it in a different character's POV. Did it change the scene? What did you learn?

How To Change Point of View

Again, if you're writing only one POV throughout your novel there won't be any need to change to a different point of view character. But if you have more than one POV character you're going to want to learn how and when to switch point of view.

Changing POV In Dual First Person POV

If you have dual first person point of views the best way to make the change is at a chapter break. It can also be done using scene breaks, but the issue with using scene breaks instead of chapter breaks is that it can be difficult to cue the reader to the change in POV. Both characters in first person are the *I* character—I went to the store, I love summer—so there's no way in a scene break to make it clear to the reader whose head we're in. I recommend using chapter breaks to let the reader know they're now with a different character.

Here's an example of using a chapter break to change POV from my novel ***Vindicate***:

Chapter One

Cora

I got my driver's license on my sixteenth birthday so I could visit my brother in prison. California Institute for Men in Chino, California sounds like one of those super snooty colleges you have to be rich to get into or else be the next generation in a long line of alumni. But this is no college. Chino Men's, as it's referred to, is one of the most violent prisons in the state.

That's where they sent my brother to serve out his life sentence.

I put the character's name in bold right after the chapter number to signal to the reader who's speaking. That way I didn't have to have the character say her name for the reader, which is really, *really* awkward in first person. Chapter two is told from a different first person POV character. Here's how I made the switch:

Chapter Two

Leo

The phone hasn't stopped ringing since my dad was interviewed on NPR. Mostly it's a lot of people wanting to get out of traffic tickets, child support, and probation. An occasional sob story gets thrown in the mix now and then, and I can see Dad wanting to help, but the fact is, he can't pay Savannah, Al, Jerry, himself, and me if every case he takes on, we do for free.

Using this technique makes the change in point of view smooth for the reader. There's no ambiguity and the reader isn't thrown out of the story.

Changing POV In Dual Third Person POV

Signaling a point of view change in third person can be done in one of three ways—at a chapter break, a hard scene break or—the most difficult way—with a new paragraph within the scene. The later technique requires a fair amount of skill to pull off cleanly without leaving the reader struggling to catch up.

Here's an example of changing point of view with a new paragraph in a scene from my novel **Rush**:

"I'm fine," she said, then again more

forcibly. "I'm fine." She repeated it like a mantra inside her head, hoping if she said it enough times it might actually become true.

Lucas risked a sideways glance at Mi to be sure. She hadn't resisted when he forced her head down and had stayed down until he let her up. She looked a little shaken, but otherwise okay. At least she wasn't crying.

By starting the second paragraph with Lucas's name I clearly signaled to the reader that I'm changing the point of view from Mi to Lucas. This technique works best with only two point of view characters. If you have more than two POV characters you're going to want to use a different technique such as a chapter break or a hard scene break.

Let's take a look at what a point of view change using a hard scene break would look like between two third person POV characters.

From my novel ***A Deep and Dark December***:

This was why Graham couldn't wait to get out of San Ray. He studied Erin. And wondered why if she had this supposed ability, she'd kept it a secret all these years. "Goddamned small town." And then he realized he'd answered his own question right there.

*****

Erin inwardly sighed. Keith really was a nice guy. She wished all over again that she could like him more. Guys who would overlook her aunt's quirkiness and offer to bail her out of jail weren't thick on the ground.

Some readers prefer the hard scene break over the paragraph POV transition. This is a personal preference you really shouldn't concern yourself with. You're not going to please all of your readers all of the time. If you're just starting out as a new writer, choose the technique that you like best as a reader and go from there. I would challenge you to learn and get good at both techniques though.

As a side note, hard scene breaks are also used to move time forward and/or change locations in a novel, which is probably why some readers prefer the paragraph technique over the hard scene break.

Here's an example from my novel **Lush** of using a hard scene break to not only change point of view, but also location:

As if sensing Lucy was nearly to her

breaking point, both the check-engine light and gas light came on at the same time. She dropped her head on the steering wheel and burst into tears.

*****

Cal poured himself a whiskey neat, propped his bare feet on his desk in his home office, and turned on the TV to the business report. He turned the volume up to drown out the rain beating against the windows. This was the way he wound down most of his days.

We go from being with Lucy in her car to being with Cal in his home. Using the paragraph technique in this instance would be very confusing to the reader as the two characters aren't in the same place at the same time.

I want to take a moment to note that how you signal a point of view change may come down to house style, meaning your publisher can dictate which technique you will use in the final draft of your published novel. If you're independently published you will want to set up your own house style with your editor and use it as a guide for all of your books. If you're unpublished you can use whichever technique you feel most confident and are most skilled at using.

Pay close attention to how other authors change point of view and learn from them. Experiment with what works best for *your* story, but be prepared to have an editor come in and tell you to make changes. That's why I recommend that you study, practice, and get good at *both* techniques. Plus it just makes you a stronger writer and gives you more tools in your authorial toolbox. And who doesn't want that?

Changing POV In Multiple Third Person POVs

If your story requires the point of view of multiple characters, changing point of view in the next paragraph won't work. You're going to have to either start a new chapter with the new POV character or use a hard scene break.

To distinguish the voice of your villain or antagonist from the voices or your protagonists I recommend doing so with a new chapter. The chapter doesn't have to be long. I've read books with chapters as short as one sentence or a paragraph or two in the villain's POV. Separating the villain's point of view this way can have a powerful impact on your story.

Be as clear as possible about which of

your characters is speaking. A good critique partner or group can help you make sure your POV changes are well defined. If there's any question in their minds about which of your characters is speaking, you may want to take a look at how you can make the point of view change as obvious as possible. Changing point of view is not where you want to get creative or reinvent the wheel. The last thing you want to do is to make your book harder to read and frustrate your reader by being too clever. Trust me on this.

How Often to Change Point of View

When it comes to point of view shifts: Less is more.

The longer you remain in a character's POV the more attached the reader gets to the character. This is especially important for your protagonists or your hero and heroine. Make the change only when it helps the story. You don't want your readers to get the feeling that they're watching a tennis match. Flip-flopping back and forth every couple of paragraphs doesn't give your reader a chance to become invested in your characters.

As I said, the longer a reader spends in the head and heart of a character the deeper the connection to that character grows. You want this. You want your reader to be fully invested in your characters and their story. You don't want to wrench them away too soon or too often. I'm not going to give a rule of thumb or page or paragraph count for how often to change point of view because each story is different.

Changing point of view can affect the pace of the whole novel so make those changes purposefully and mindfully. Know why you need to be in a particular character's POV at this point in your book before making the switch. What does changing the point of view add to the scene? How will it move the story forward? What new information is gleaned? If you have well-defined answers to those questions, then make the switch.

Exercise:

Write a short scene and switch point of view in the middle of it. Try it first with a scene break and then rewrite it and change POV in a new paragraph. This will only work in third person. Which technique did you like best? Did the exercise make you want to change how you normally change POV?

Common Point of View Violations

Some of the most common POV violations I have seen in work I've critiqued and in contests I've judged are:

James entered the parking garage and moved toward his car, his mind on the meeting he'd just left. Something moved in the shadows. James jerked back in surprise. Unaware, his hold on his keys relaxed, and he dropped them.

Okay, if James isn't *consciously aware* that his hold relaxed then it's a violation to make him simultaneously *aware* that he dropped his keys. Remember, the reader should only be shown what the character knows *when they know it*.

Let's rewrite this passage in deep POV:

James stepped off the elevator of the parking garage, his boss's words a constant loop in his head—you're fired. What was he going to do? Yesterday he'd been so thrilled to find out he was going to be a father. Today he was not only out of a job, but also health insurance. A shadow moved into his peripheral view. James jerked back, preparing to strike. A sound like a gunshot echoed in the cavernous garage. He dropped to the ground and listened. Nothing. Just a car coming down from the level above. Something bit into his abdomen. He rolled to find that he'd dropped his keys, then fell on them. He shook his head at his stupidity and stood up to brush himself off.

See the difference? Action (a shadow moved) → Reaction (James jerked back) → Awareness (something bit into his abdomen).

Let's try another one:

As Sally walked home from school she didn't notice that Bobby was following her.

If she didn't notice him, then he wasn't there. Remember, you can only give your reader the information that your character *knows*. Now for the rewrite using deep point of view:

Sally walked her usual route home from school. Bright color from Mrs. Miller's yard caught her eye. Roses! Pink roses. Her favorite. Bending over the fence to smell them, a prickling sensation crept up her back. She turned to find Bobby standing just feet behind her. Where had he come from? What did he want?

Using phrases like *little did she know* or *he didn't realize it but* or *she didn't notice that* are what's called author intrusion where the author uses their all-seeing eye to give the reader information that the point of view character doesn't have.

Another POV violation I see a lot from new writers is:

Wendy's cheeks flushed.

If we're in Wendy's POV she can't see her cheeks flush unless she's looking in a mirror. She can *feel* her face grow hot, but she can't *see* it. Another violation I see often is:

Wendy's eyes flashed in anger.

or

Wendy's eyes glowed with amusement.

Again, if we're in Wendy's POV she's not going to know what her eyes look like unless she's viewing herself in a mirror. She can narrow her eyes in anger or widen her eyes in amusement because that's a motion she can control and feel. There's no confusion about whose point of view we're in.

Speaking of confusing POV...

Read the following passage and then see if you can figure out whose point of view this scene is in.

"I promise to always keep you safe, Sally." He instinctively holds me tighter, wrapping me in his warmth.

I've never felt safer or more loved.

If you guessed Sally's, you're correct...and incorrect. The word *instinctively* confuses the POV. If we're in Sally's point of view how does she know what his instinct is? By deleting that one word the POV is strengthened and there's no doubt at all that we're firmly in Sally's point of view.

Head Hopping

Editors cite head hopping as something new authors do without realizing they've done it. In the last chapter we talked about changing point of view and how often to do it and I warned to not create scenes where the reader feels like they're watching a tennis match. We'll explore exactly what that means in this section.

To be clear, head hopping is not simply a change in point of view from one character to another. It's when that change happens in the middle of a sentence or paragraph and occurs multiple times in a scene. The switch often happens without the writer consciously making the choice.

Here's an example of head hopping mid sentence:

He felt her stare and she thought he was handsome.

We're going to ignore how bulky the

sentence is and all of the telling—he felt, she thought—and focus on the two different points of view in the example. If we're in his head feeling her stare, then we can't know she thought he was handsome at the same time. See the confusion?

Let's try another one. This time we'll head hop back and forth in a short scene:

Jenna sipped the bitter coffee and surveyed the passersby in the street. She checked her watch again. He was late. He was always late.

As soon as he entered the café he saw her. She had her back to him, people watching as usual. Even from behind he could read her mood. She was irritated, probably with him for being late.

She felt him as soon as he walked in, but didn't turn around. Let him come to her for a change instead of the other way around. He owed her that much after everything he'd put her through.

Did you spot the point of view switches? I changed point of view in each paragraph. Felt a bit like a ping-pong match, didn't it? Be ever vigilant in maintaining point of view. Make your POV switches thoughtful and deliberate. Don't get caught making a rooky head hopping mistakes.

When the author moves the camera from one point of view character to another, the perspective also changes. The reader then gets to experience the author's world from this new character's point of view. Changing the point of view from one character to another can give the reader information that the other characters in the story might not have, such as why Bobby is following Sally or why Wendy's eyes are flashing in anger. The reader will know things that the other characters don't know. This technique can be used to great effect.

Readers want to be in the know. They want a shot at guessing whom the murderer is, knowing what really happened on *the night that changed everything* or what the characters are hiding from one another. When the reader is given extra information from other POV characters, they're involved in the story on a deeper level. It gives them a stake in what happens and a curiosity to keep reading to see how the story will play out. This is exactly what you want for your story.

Male vs. Female Point of View

Please bear with me as I speak generally on this topic. I fully understand that not everyone fits into assigned gender roles and that emotions, life experiences, expectations, etc. can affect how a person will react, how they feel, and what they might do or say. I dislike stereotypes so it pains me a bit to lump all males into one category and all females into another. But here goes...

Men generally use shorter, to the point sentences. When recalling events they're likely to give you just the facts, ma'am. The more emotional a situation is, the more likely men are to close themselves off to get control of their emotions. They can sometimes react angrily. They're not long on description and details. This doesn't mean nothing's going on inside their heads. On the contrary, I've found that men can think very deep thoughts and experience a great range of emotions. They just might not show it.

Women tend to use longer, more

descriptive sentences. They give more detail and may even assign emotions to objects or events. They relay a lot of information, often more than what the other person asked for. Women tend to be apologetic about their perceived inadequacies and may defer to men or to other women who they deem more powerful than them. They more openly show emotion and are willing to talk about those emotions.

As an example, a man might say 'The house is blue.' Whereas a woman might describe the house as 'light blue with dark blue trim, with gingerbread around the porch, and a red roof.' Unless the man was an architect or remodeled houses for a living or as a hobby. In that case he might go into more detail about the house because of his profession.

Men don't express emotion outwardly as often or in the same ways as women do. Being in your male character's POV during an emotional moment for him will give your reader greater insight into him as a character, as well as the scene. Your hero can act like a jerk toward the heroine, but the reader will forgive him because they know how what's happening in the scene is affecting him and why he's behaving the way he is.

I once read the work in progress of a friend. In the scene her hero was acting like a real jerk toward the heroine, really being rude. The scene was written from the heroine's point of view. This was the first time the hero appeared on the page so I didn't know anything about him and why he was being so despicable to my precious heroine who I'd just spent eight or so pages falling in love with. I knew he was supposed to be her one true love, but all I wanted her to do was turn her back on him and leave. In short, I hated him.

In my comments to my friend I suggested she rewrite the scene from the hero's point of view. She did and what a difference a POV change made. I not only understood why he behaved the way he did toward the heroine, I also got a peek into their history together. He was mad at her for jilting him. I could've gotten the same info from the heroine's point of view, but it didn't have the same emotional impact coming from her. I needed to understand not only his anger, but how deeply she'd hurt him.

Stepping out of gender stereotypes can create fascinating and unique characters and scenes. A hero who gets misty-eyed during those awful abused animal commercials and yet can dig a bullet out of his own thigh without painkillers would make for an interesting, multi-dimensional character. A heroine who hates to shop for clothes and shoes, but gets excited about buying power tools because she knows how to use them would be a nice twist on the gender norm. Draw complex, multi-faceted characters with deep backstories, then give them a plot they can sink their teeth into. Make sure their actions and reactions are consistent with who they are and who they want to be.

What Is Deep Point of View?

Now that we've learned about the different kinds of point of view, when and how to switch POV, and common point of view mistakes, let's go deep into point of view. Deep point of view is achieved when the writer so fully immerses herself and the reader into the character's head and heart that the writer virtually disappears, drawing the reader deeper into the story.

Uh-huh. Okay. *But how do I do that?*

Let's break it down into chunks, then we'll put it all back together.

Show Don't Tell

If you've taken any online classes, read a book or two on writing or attended writers workshops or conferences, then you've probably heard this term bandied about quite a bit. But what does it mean?

As Anton Chekhov said, "Don't tell me the moon is shining; show me the glint of light on broken glass."

Showing creates vivid images in your reader's mind. It inserts your reader directly into the scene right along with your character as if they inhabit the same body. You want your reader to cry when your character despairs and laugh when he's amused.

Telling summarizes what is happening for the reader. It's a statement or synopsis about what is happening to a character in the scene. Kind of like a book report. It creates distance between your reader and your story.

Showing and telling do essentially the same thing—relay information to the reader. But *showing* draws the reader in, while *telling* creates a buffer or distance between your character and your reader. Readers want to *experience* a story, not be *told* about it. Showing requires descriptive words and phrases to draw mental pictures for your reader and invoke their emotions whereas telling is just the facts, ma'am.

News reporters and nonfiction authors *tell* you what is happening.

Movie directors and fiction authors *show* you.

Showing requires more words than *telling* and is much more illustrative and theatrical. You're baking a cake, experiencing all of the sights, sounds, and smells, not reciting a cake recipe while holding up a photo of a cake. See the difference?

Not to confuse things, but there will be times when you will want to *tell* to move the story along. You can't *show* everything or your book will be a gazillion and one pages long. Be mindful and purposeful about it. And please, please, *please* keep it short. Switch back into showing as soon as possible.

Ever read a book where the author described everything the character did in excruciating detail? He woke up. He brushed his teeth. He took a shower. He got dressed.... Move it along already! That stuff's boring. No one cares about it. It's okay to tell the reader he got ready for work and then jump into the scene where his chatty neighbor who's really into him waylays him in the hall. That last bit is waaayyy more interesting than his dental hygiene. Trust me on this.

Show vs. tell often comes down to word choice. Word choice matters. Tattoo this on the inside of your forehead because you'll want to keep it at the front of your mind at all times while writing and editing. Word choice can be the difference between a reader throwing your book at the wall or placing it lovingly on their keeper shelf. It might sound silly, but I've spent considerable time trying to decide between *of* and *the* in a sentence. Way more times than I'm willing to admit even to myself. Word choice matters that much.

Telling Words

Telling words filter the reader's experience rather than drawing them into the story. Words like felt, saw, heard, and thought *tell* the reader what is happening.

An example of telling:

Bob thought his coworkers were jerks. They kept stealing his lunch. He felt picked on.

Whoop-dee-do. Bob's lunch-stealing coworkers made him feel picked on. We're *told* about his emotions. Why should we care? This passage doesn't make us *feel* his annoyance. We're distanced from Bob and his missing lunch. Let's try it again this time we'll *show* how Bob feels when he finds his lunch missing.

An example of showing:

Gone. Again. The boiling hot rage that had been simmering all week rose and rose until the white of the refrigerator's interior turned deep red and his head pounded. Someone had stolen his lunch for the fifth time in as many days. That was it. No more Mr. Nice Guy.

In the second example we're deep into

Bob's point of view—we're in his head, hearing his thoughts as if they are our own. We *feel* Bob's anger at having his lunch stolen. There's no buffer between him and us. We're fully immersed in his point of view.

Pronouns and Proper Names

If you find yourself using a lot of proper names and pronouns when describing, you're probably using them alongside telling words- *Scott* felt, *Cindy* saw, *they* heard, and so on. As in our previous example with Bob and his coworkers— *Bob* thought his coworkers were jerks. *He* felt picked on. Using a lot of pronouns and proper names separates your reader from your characters and you never want to do that. The closer you can bring your reader to your characters, the better. Draw them into the story and make them never want to leave.

Active Verbs vs Passive and Inactive Verbs

Passive and inactive verbs are sneaky. They can creep into your work without you even realizing it. They assist where oftentimes no help is needed. They're a sure sign of a new or lazy writer. And you're not a lazy writer, are you?

Keep It Active

Active verbs are the combo meal in description—they're action with a side of adjective. Active verbs do more than show what your character is doing; they describe how your character is doing it. Make sure you're using the most active verbs you can in your description.

He held the baby. **vs.** He cradled the baby.

Cradled does more than show what he's doing with the baby, it shows how he might feel about the baby.

She went into the house. **vs.** She stormed into the house.

Stormed gives the reader insight into her emotional state as she enters the house and she's probably not happy.

In these two examples the word choices of *cradled* and *stormed* are doing double duty. They show what is happening and give insight into the character's feelings. Make sure to use the strongest verb you can think of. Whenever possible choose verbs that will work hard for you in the sentence.

Passive and Inactive Verbs

If you find yourself putting words such as is, are, am, was, were, be, being, been, do, does, did, has, have, had, might, or may before verbs—you're using *passive verbs* or passive voice.

Example of passive: Becky was going to the store.

Was about to... maybe she will, maybe she won't. We don't know and likely we don't care.

The excessive use of passive verbs is the most telling sign of a beginning writer. Overusing passive verbs is flat out lazy writing. Don't cheat yourself and don't cheat your reader. Before turning your manuscript in to your editor or agent or entering it in a contest, do a final round editing pass to look for passive verbs and weed them out wherever you can.

Inactive verbs such as started to, began to, proceeded to, could, would, there was, there are, there is, there were, seemed to, tried to—dilute the verb you're using.

Example of inactive: Becky started to go to the store.

She *started* to go, but we don't really know if she went or not. Be sure this ambiguity is what you want to convey before using inactive verbs. A good example of when you'd want to use an inactive verb is: Becky started to go to the store, but Julie called her back.

Example of active: Becky went to the store.

She went... she's already gone. See the difference?

Will there be times when you'll want to use passive or inactive verbs? Yes, of course. I'm not telling you not to. But if you do a search and you find that you have an excessive amount of 'was going's' or 'started to's' in your manuscript, you may want to look at your verb choices and make some changes. Use inactive and passive verbs sparingly and purposefully.

Using the Five Senses to Achieve Deep POV

Using the five senses—scent, sight, sound, touch, taste—in description grounds the reader in the scene. Sensory description enriches the reader experience, especially when tied to things the reader would be familiar with—the smell of fresh baked cookies, the sound of a heart beat, the sight of a beautiful sunset, the touch of a mother's hand, the tart taste of an apple.

As E.L. Doctorow said, "Good writing is supposed to evoke sensation in the reader—not the fact that it is raining, but the feeling of being rained upon."

Sight

Most novels (with the exception of children's books) lack photos or drawings to give the reader a visual. It's up to you, the writer, to draw those pictures with your words. Creating vivid visual imagery is very important in deep point of view. In fact, it's the one element writers think of most when creating their world for the reader. But humans don't experience the world by sight alone. We have four other senses that feed us information and help us navigate through our day-to-day lives. Vision is just one way we assimilate information about all manner of things from the weather, a location, a building, an object or a person.

A visual description alone is not enough to draw the reader into your scene. What if it's too dark for your character to see anything? What if your character is blind? How would that character describe his world? Challenge yourself to not rely solely on visuals to draw your reader deeper into your story. It's your job to help them experience *every* aspect of your world.

Scent

Smell is the most nostalgic of the senses and can help your reader identify with your character in unexpected ways. With scent you can call up past experiences and memories for your character and your reader—the smell of a father's aftershave, the scent of freshly mowed grass, the aroma of Grandma's apple pie—you get the idea. It's all very sentimental and can be a moment of shared experience between your reader and your point of view character.

Sound

Unless your character is experiencing sound deprivation or is deaf, there will be noise in his world. In fact, the absence of sound in a setting can give your character and your reader a sense that something is very wrong—a jungle that goes suddenly quiet or the secession of chatter when a character enters a room. Comparing one sound to another in description can be very effective—the wail of an ambulance was like a child's scream in the dead of night. It creates an immediate, identifiable sound for your reader.

Use noise —whether it's ordinary or extraordinary—to lure in your reader and give them more information about your character's world.

Touch

There are two different kinds of touch—the way something *feels* and the sensation of *being touched*. Touch can be pleasurable or painful or, in some cases, a combination of both. The way something feels to your character either emotionally or physically and the comparisons they might make to past experiences can reveal things about your characters to the reader. A hot, sweaty handshake can say something about a character's emotions that a cool, dry hand can't. Using touch to draw comparisons between things can be quite interesting—a cold headstone on a sweltering summer day, for example.

How a character reacts to being touched physically is a great way to tap into emotions that can have roots in a character's backstory. Does your character like being touched or are they uncomfortable with it? Is your character the touchy-feely type or do they use touch sparingly with meaning? Touch is a very important sense in sex scenes. It can elevate the scene from playful to deeply sensual, depending on the type of touch.

Taste

Taste is most often used when a character is eating and drinking or kissing and making love—occasions when they'll be using their mouths and tongues. There are other, more unexpected times when you can use the sense of taste—the coppery, metallic taste of blood, a salty ocean breeze, the mouthwatering expectation of your mother's meatloaf. Look for unexpected ways to use taste in place of one of the other senses to show your reader more.

The Sixth Sense

The unscientific sixth sense can be used to foreshadow events or alert a character to something wrong that could protect them from danger. Don't confuse this sense with an omniscient point of view. Make sure your character is experiencing this sense and you're not intruding as an author.

Little did Mary know, but a bad guy was hiding around the corner.

The above is not an example of using the sixth sense and it's not an example of omniscient point of view. The author has inserted himself into the scene by giving the reader information that only the author—not Mary—knows. Please don't confuse author intrusion with omniscient POV or the sixth sense. Let's try it again and see if you can discern the difference.

The fine hairs on Mary's neck stood on end and she had the uncomfortable sensation of being watched.

The physical sensation of *the fine hairs on Mary's neck standing on end* is not only an example of the sixth sense, it's also a terrific way to draw your reader into your character's experience. We get the strong feeling that something is wrong at the same time Mary does. We're fully immersed in her POV. It could be a bad guy hiding around the corner or it could be a raccoon watching her. As a reader we don't know and that's okay. What happens next will fill in the blanks for the reader. The most important thing is that you let your reader experience what happens to the character *as it's happening*.

Using More Than One Sense to Deepen POV

Using more than one sense in a scene can have a powerful effect and deepen the reader's experience. Try to employ at least two—if not or more—of the five senses in your scenes. This isn't a license to bust out all five senses in one scene. Think about how you experience your world. If you're bombarded with information from every single one of your senses at once with no way to pick and choose the most important, your brain would likely shut down. It's the same for your reader.

Here are some examples of using more than one sense in a scene and the powerful emotions you can conjure in your characters and your reader.

From *How to Bake a Perfect Life* by

Barbara O'Neal:

A collection of blue bottles, large and small, was lined up on the windowsill. Sandwiched between them were small clay pots filled with herbs. When the sun was on them, like now, they made the air smell like root beer and Thanksgiving morning.

In this scene, Ms. O'Neal not only gives the reader a visual, she creates an evocative scent to ground the reader. We all know what Thanksgiving and root beer smell like, but put together we really begin to picture the windowsill and the room, coloring in the scene with our own emotions and scent memories.

From ***Vindicate*** by Beth Yarnall:

When he's close like this I forget why things could never work out between us. His scent wraps around me in the small space. I breathe him in and it's like he's a part of me. The stroke of his thumb across my cheek echoes in other parts of my body and I feel myself leaning into him like a flower seeks the sun. I don't want any of this and yet it's all *I want.*

Here we have scent combined with touch,

which is often used in love scenes. We're naturally drawn to a mate whose DNA is very different than ours and one of the ways we do that is through smelling the pheromones they give off. It's an inborn instinct to ensure our offspring are the strongest and healthiest they can be.

According to Desmond Morris's ***Intimate Behaviour: A Zoologist's Classic Study of Human Intimacy***, there are twelve levels of intimacy that escalate from one (eye to body glance) to twelve (intercourse). A hand to face touch is a level eight on the intimacy scale and is considered more intimate than a kiss, which clocks in at level seven. So in this scene we've got a pretty powerful touch combined with a very strong reaction to scent. A one-two punch.

As you can see from these examples, using the senses can enhance the reader experience and draw them deeper into your scenes.

Visceral or Physical Reactions in Deep POV

Emotions often evoke physical or visceral reactions such as a pounding heart, sweating hands or a sick stomach. Using physical reactions to emotions shows the reader what your character is feeling without you having to tell the reader what your character is feeling and experiencing.

Shallow POV:

She heard his footsteps on the stairs. What to do? She threw the latch on the door and backed away from it. She was going to be in for it this time.

Meh. This scene just sort of lies there on the page. We're not emotionally invested in what happens when he reaches the top of the stairs. We have no real sense of who these people are and what their relationship is.

There's also a lot of telling in this scene. Did you catch it? *She heard, she* threw the latch, *she was going to* be in for it—it's all telling and no showing. I can do better and so can you.

Now we're going to take the same number of sentences (four) and rewrite the passage in deep point of view.

Deep POV:

The thud of his boots on the stairs pounded in her ears. Her heart fluttered like a captured bird in her chest as she frantically wondered what to do. With numbed fingers she threw the latch on the door and backed away from it, prickles of dread racing up her spine. She was going to be in for it this time.

We're genuinely worried for her, aren't we? We can feel her growing fear with every sentence. We're concerned about what's going to happen to her when he reaches the top of the stairs. We don't know what the relationship is between the two of them exactly, but we know that it isn't good.

Here's another example of shallow POV:
Jenny didn't like spiders. She thought they were gross.

VISCERAL OR PHYSICAL REACTIONS IN DEEP POV

Okay, we get that Jenny doesn't like spiders. So what? This passage doesn't make us feel Jenny's revulsion. It's blah. Boring. There's also more telling—*Jenny* didn't like, *she thought*. Those pesky proper names and pronouns rear their ugly heads again along with the telling word—thought. I hope you're starting to see the pattern here and are beginning to discern telling from showing. Let's try again without all of the filtering.

Example of deep POV:

Spiders had to be the most disgusting creatures. All those hairy legs skittering about. Anything that moved like that had to be up to no good.

In the second example we're deep into Jenny's point of view—we're in her head, hearing her thoughts as if they are our own. We can *feel* her revulsion. There's no buffer between Jenny and us. We're fully immersed in her point of view. You can almost feel the creepy crawly legs too, can't you?

From ***Dark Wild Night*** by Christina Lauren:
The memory trips a fluttery, anxious beat

in my chest.

This is a great, non-clichéd version of a pounding heart. Whenever possible try to be original in your writing of emotion.

From ***Vindicate*** by Beth Yarnall:

"God, Cora." His voice is a sigh that arrows straight through me, fanning out into tiny prickles of pleasure and pain.

The sigh doesn't literally pierce her body, but we get a very clear picture of the effect that the tone of his voice has on her emotionally, which manifests physically. A double whammy. Be original (am I starting to sound like a broken record?) in your comparisons. Make the reader feel what your character is feeling as they're feeling it.

From ***Dark Wild Night*** by Christina Lauren:

I never want to run out of clothes because every time he peels something away, he kisses me lower, hums against the skin, and bites just the smallest bit. It's like having lust uncorked and poured in bubbly streams across my skin.

A terrific description of the physical

manifestation of arousal, isn't it? You can imagine what *bubbly streams* might feel like when poured across your skin. Very original.

As the author James Michener said, "I love writing. I love the swirl and swing of words as they tangle with human emotions."

Get your readers' emotions tangled in *your* writing. Make them *feel* your words. A reader won't put down a book or throw it across the room because it makes them *feel* too much. I promise. Cross-my-heart-hope-to-die *promise*. Emotion is the hook you'll use to pull your reader through your story from chapter one to The End. Don't cheat and don't pull your punches. Go there. Go all the way there with emotion. You know you've done your job when you write a scene that scares you and makes you worry that you've gone too far. You haven't. You can't.

Internal Dialog and Introspection in Deep Point of View

Internal thoughts must be written in the POV character's point of view. In other words, stay in your character's head if you're writing the scene in his point of view. It seems obvious but you wouldn't believe how many times writers—sometimes seasoned writers—get this wrong. Giving your reader access to your character's deepest thoughts can have a powerful effect on your story, but make sure it advances the plot. Your character mentally waxing philosophical on the relevance of anarchism in modern society while trying to figure out how the bad guy did it isn't going to serve your plot or your reader. Make your words count, even unspoken words.

Achieving Deep Point of View in Internal Dialog and Introspection

The point of deep point of view is to insert your

reader into the head and heart of your characters. Internal dialog and introspection is a great way to achieve that. Obviously, character introspection puts your reader inside your character's brain. The reader is privy to all of the character's thoughts and insights. So clearly it's easy to achieve deep point of view, right?

Not necessarily.

But, but the reader is in my character's head. You just said so!

Well, yeah, I did, but feeding your character's thoughts directly to your reader doesn't automatically mean you're employing deep point of view. All the rules like *show don't tell* and *author intrusion* still apply and you wouldn't believe how easy it is to break those rules in internal dialog and introspection. Let me give you an example.

A man approached, but he wasn't wearing a white coat. I wonder if he's the doctor, *she thought.*

Two things are going on here:

1) When we wonder about something we don't think *I wonder*. We just have the thought. Using the word *wonder* distances the reader from your character.

2) There are no dialog tags in thoughts. Dialog tags are for dialog—when a

INTERNAL DIALOG AND INTROSPECTION

character is speaking out loud. That's why they're called *dialog* tags.

I should also note that there are no quotation marks in internal dialog. Quotation marks are for *spoken* dialog, not for words that stay in the character's head.

Let's rewrite that passage, following the rules we've been talking about all book long.

A man approached, but he wasn't wearing a white coat. Was he the doctor? *He certainly carried himself like one.*

With the italicized words being opposite in this book than they would be in your book, things can get a little confusing. So I'm going to give it to you again exactly as you would write it.

A man approached, but he wasn't wearing a white coat. *Was he the doctor?* He certainly carried himself like one.

The internal thought or internal dialog would be italicized. The rest of the passage would not be. By italicizing *Was he the doctor?* and not using the dialog tag *she thought* the reader gets the character's thoughts straight from the character's head. There's no filter. The two sentences bracketing the thought—A man approached, but he wasn't wearing a white coat. and He certainly carried himself like one.—are action and description, *not* internal thought.

The question is the only thought.

Let's try another one.

He felt the pain of the knife piercing his thigh and wondered how he could've been so wrong about her.

More *wondering*. Bad writer! There's also some filtering or telling going on with *he felt the pain*. Your reader should clutch their thigh at the imagined sensation of a knife stabbing into *their* leg just as it pierces your character's leg. They're not going to feel it with this passage. Let's try that again. This time I'm going to write it the way you would in your novel.

White-hot fire shot through his thigh. He glanced down. The polished hilt of a knife sticking out of his leg glinted back at him. The bitch had stabbed him. *How could I have been so wrong about her?*

The filter is gone and we're experiencing what's happening to him as it's happening. Sensation (pain) → Realization (he's been stabbed) → Thought (question). We're deep in his point of view, getting the information about what's happening to him *as it's happening*. Note the use of *I* in the question—How could *I* have been so wrong about her? Switching from the pronoun *he* to *I* is a dead giveaway that this is internal dialog.

What if your character is psychic? How

would you show internal dialog that is shared telepathically with another character and still stay in deep point of view? With the use of dialog tags.

Whoa. Hold up. You just said not to use dialog tags in internal thought.

Yup. I sure did. But in this case the internal thought is *also* dialog—unspoken dialog, but dialog all the same and you'll want to make that clear for your reader. Here's how you can do that:

He's lying, I said telepathically to my brother. *The corner of his eye always twitches when he lies.*

You could replace *I said telepathically to my brother* with *I mentally told my brother* or something else along those lines. By italicizing the internal dialog, but not italicizing the dialog tag, you're signaling to the reader that these are words that are not spoken out loud. Remember, there are no quotation marks in internal dialog.

When to Use Internal Dialog and Introspection

Showing your character's emotional vulnerability can help your reader more easily identify with your character, help them to understand your character's goals and the motivation behind them, and make them fall in love with your character—even with a seemingly unlikeable character like the villain. If you're getting feedback that your reader is having a hard time liking or identifying with your character you might want to look at how much time you're spending in his or her head. If the answer is not much, then take a look at how you can change that.

Readers want *real* characters they can identify with and root for. Vulnerability is one of the most important characteristics you can give your characters. By making your character emotionally vulnerable you make him or her more accessible to your reader. Reveal your character's emotional depth by exposing his deepest, most intimate thoughts and insecurities. Your character's fear, uncertainty, hope, unhappiness, joy, disappointment, dreams, anger, sorrow, longing, and endurance in the face of adversity are opportunities for your reader to connect and empathize with your character.

Use introspection during and/or after your most highly charged emotional scenes to build that reader connection. Giving your reader access to your character's thoughts and emotions during and/or just after emotional scenes will help build empathy and emotional attachment between your reader and your characters. This is also a great time to reveal your character's motivation and help your reader to understand why your character is reacting the way they are in the scene. Why is she afraid? What does she want and why does she want it? What is he hiding? Why is he angry? What's the motivation behind her revenge? Giving your reader a peek into your character's motivation and deepest thoughts and emotions will keep your reader turning the pages.

Use introspection and internal dialog to show character growth. Your hero should not be the same man at the end of the book that he was in the beginning. The plot events and emotional upheaval your character will go through throughout the story should force your character to struggle, change, and come out the other side a new man.

Sometimes a character is hiding a deep, dark secret that they can't share with any of the other characters in the novel. Internal thought is a great way to give your reader more and expose those truths at times when your character is vulnerable or put to the test. The reader is invested in the expectation of when and how the secret will be exposed and what will happen to the character when it's finally revealed to the other character/s. It's a chance for your reader to worry about your character and root for him.

Have you ever heard the term scene and sequel? Scene is where the action and dialog occurs. Sequel is introspection and internal dialog. A sequel occurring after a dramatic or emotionally intense scene is a chance for you to slow the pace of the novel and to let the characters and your reader take a breath to examine where they were and where they are now. It's an opportunity for your character to think things through, sort out a new course of action, and come to a conclusion on what to do next. It's a resting spot in the novel. Without it your book would be nonstop tension.

But I'm writing an intense thriller. I *want* a lot of tension.

All novels have tension, but strung too tight over too long a period of time the reader will unconsciously look for a way to relieve some of it. It usually manifests as a laugh that the reader has no control over. Humans can't handle stress and strain over extended periods of time. Their psyche will look for ways to let off a little steam and it will probably occur at a place in your novel where you don't want your reader to laugh. Pull back on the emotional reins every now and then. Give your reader room to breath before ratcheting up the tension again.

You should be layering your novel with scenes and sequels that move the plot forward. Stick to the rules of deep point of view and your reader should have no problem identifying with and falling in love with your characters.

Deep Point of View in Dialog

Using deep point of view in dialog is the perfect place to give your reader little slices of insight into who your characters are. Dialog tags and brief moments of introspection and internal dialog are little pockets where you can show your reader more about your character, her emotional state, her opinions, and her relationship to the person or persons she's speaking with. Never miss an opportunity to slip in added tension, emotion, and subtext into your story.

Uh, hey, wait. What's subtext?

Subtext is unspoken dialog—the meaning behind your character's words. Have you ever been a part of a conversation that on the surface appeared to be about one thing, but was really about something else altogether? That's subtext. It's subtle and not always easy to achieve.

Here's an example of subtext from my novel, ***A Deep and Dark December***:

"It's good to see you like this."

She lowered her arms, but didn't spin around. Somehow she knew he'd come or he'd known she would come. Either way, here they were.

She turned around slowly, bracing herself to see him up close for the first time in weeks. Her preparation was wasted. Nothing could've prepared her for the sight of him as wet as she, standing just a few feet away.

"It's good to feel like this," she answered.

He cocked his head to the side, a small smile tilting up one corner of his mouth. "Nice weather we're having."

She tucked her hands in her coat pockets and gave him the same sort of smile in return. "Isn't it?"

"I've heard if you count one-Mississippi, two-Mississippi after a lightning strike, you can tell how close a storm is. Four-Mississippi would be four miles away."

"Is it important to you to know how far away a storm is?"

"It's important for me to know where I stand in nature. It can turn on a dime."

She nodded. "Hmm, I've heard that. Do you think by predicting how far away a storm is that you can know for certain when it will reach you?"

"Maybe. If I've done all the right things in the right way for the right reasons." He looked up at the sky as lightning flashed. "One-Mississippi, two-Mississippi, three-Mississippi, four-Mississip—"

In four short steps she crashed into him. They held each other hard as though the storm would sweep them out to sea. She tilted her face up, he met her halfway, and they kissed a slow, winding kiss that spun her world on its axis. It had been so long since she'd been with him. So long since she'd felt him, *so long* since the scent of him wrapped around her.

Holding her face in his hands, he broke the kiss and stared down at her. "They also say that storms wash everything clean. Do you believe that?"

"I think that's quite possible, depending on how strong it is."

"What about one as strong as this one?"

She glanced up as another flash of light streaked the sky. "One-Mississippi, two-Miss—" Thunder roared.

Graham's heart beat nearly as loud as the thunder. "It's almost on top of us."

She nodded, her face sliding through his fingers, wet from the rain and her tears.

"I'm not leaving until it's right on top of us," he promised.

"Me either."

"We can keep counting as it moves on, track its progress."

"I don't think I can stay here that long."

"No?"

She shook her head. "I don't need to. I'll believe you when you tell me the worst is over."

Relief washed through him. "I can do that."

The sky blazed bright, illuminating them for a split second.

"One-Miss," they whispered together.

BOOM.

"It's here," she breathed.

Bringing her face to his chest, needing that full body connection, he held her tighter. "I've got you."

They're not just talking about the rain, are they? The storm is a metaphor for their relationship, for where they've been and where they're going. They're talking about the rain, but they're also talking about whether or not they're going to stay together. I joke that this book is my subtext book because a lot of the conversations are about something other than what the characters seem to be discussing on the surface. Look for ways to give depth to your dialog scenes with subtext.

In this section we're going to work on how to make your dialog tags disappear to the point that the reader barely notices them because he's so engrossed in the story and what's playing out on the page. Dialog is a great place to reveal new information to your reader, but beware of the *As you know Bob...* conversation. If you're not familiar with it I'll give a brief example then move on. We're talking about deep point of view, not dialog in this book, so I want to stay on course.

Here's an example:

"Why did you go to New York, Brenda?"
"Well, as you know Bob, I went to New York to visit my dying great aunt who is about to leave me ten trillion dollars, her apartment in the Dakota, and her toy poodle. She's the one who started that line of diamond-encrusted dog collars that every celebrity just had to have. She's my mother's father's sister. She never married and doesn't have any children so I'm her only heir."

Super duper info dumpy, isn't it? The information is new to the reader, but not to Bob. Find a more clever way to get the new information to your reader without falling into this dialog trap.

Dialog is also a great place to hint at and slowly disclose a secret one of your characters might be hiding. You always want to clue your reader in first that there's a secret before your other characters catch on. It's a great way to build suspense and tension in the reader and keep them turning the pages to find out when and how the secret will come out and how the other characters will react to it.

Let's take a look at a scene from my novel **Atone**. Our heroine, Vera, has a secret. Actually she has several that I feed to the reader and to the hero Beau, inch by inch. First I'll give it to you in shallow point of view and then I'll deepen it in stages until we get to how the scene was written in the final draft. The italics will be just as you'd write them in your novel. The scene is in first person point of view from Beau's POV.

Here's the first example:

"You know who this *Daddy* guy is, don't you?" I ask.

Looking away, she fidgets with the bag.

"Who is he?"

She doesn't answer as she starts to tear the bag into pieces.

"Who is he to *you*?"

"He's not anything to me."

"Who *was* he, then?"

She takes a long time to answer.

"You came here wanting our help," I tell her. "I can't help you if you withhold information from me."

"Javier Abano," she says. "I was with him when I was fourteen until . . . I wasn't anymore."

There's no real emotion in this scene, is there? We're not connected to these characters or invested in the outcome of their conversation. What are the stakes? What new information is revealed? The name of the man who goes by *Daddy*, but that's about it, right? Let's try again. This time we'll go a little bit deeper. As we go forward, pay attention to word choice, physical actions, and the introspection of the POV character. How does it change?

Here's the second example of the same scene:

"You know who this *Daddy* guy is, don't you?" I press.

Her gaze slinks away as she shreds the bag into pieces.

"Who is he?"

She doesn't answer. Her hands shake as she tears the bag.

"Who is he to *you*?"

"He's not anything to me." She wants this to be true, but it's not.

"Who *was* he, then?"

She takes a long time to decide how to answer. In the end, it comes down to whether or not she wants me to help her find her sister.

"You came here wanting our help," I remind her. "I can't help you if you withhold information from me."

"Javier Abano." Her voice is ugly and brutal. "I was with him when I was fourteen until . . . I wasn't anymore."

We're a little deeper. The first dialog tag changes from *I ask* to *I press*, showing the reader that he's having to pull the information out of her. He *reminds* her why she's there instead of *telling* her why she's there. Another clue that he has to drag the words out of her.

Her actions just sort of lie there. They don't give the POV character or the reader any insight into what she might be feeling and he doesn't seem to consider them at all as he's questioning her. Her shaking hands give us a slight indication of how she might be feeling, but she could be nervous, scared or just have low blood sugar. We really don't know. It's not enough.

Here's the scene as it was written in the final draft:

"You know who this *Daddy* guy is, don't you?" I press.

Her gaze slinks away. She fidgets with the bag, shredding it into little pieces.

"Who is he?"

She doesn't answer. Her hands shake as she tears the bag, but her shoulders are straight. She's a contradiction of stress and determination.

And then it hits me. "Who is he to *you*?"

"He's not anything to me." She wants this to be true, but it's not.

"Who *was* he, then?"

She takes a long time to decide how to answer. In the end, it comes down to whether or not she wants me to help her find her sister, and we both know it.

"You came here wanting our help," I remind her. "I can't help you if you withhold information from me."

"Javier Abano." Her voice is ugly and brutal, like it was the other night when she asked me if I wanted to fuck her. "I was with him when I was fourteen until . . . I wasn't anymore."

We don't know much about these characters from this short excerpt because I kind of plopped you into the middle of the novel. I did that on purpose. I wanted to show you a scene between the two of them that occurs during the getting-to-know-you stage of their relationship. There's more mental trying-to-figure-the-other-person-out at this point in the book than there is earlier or later so it's a great spot to play with tension, subtext, and emotion. They're interested in each other romantically and invested in each other to a certain extent.

Notice how he reads her body language and reacts to it, injecting what he already knows about her into the mix, and comes up with conclusions about what she's saying and most importantly what she's *not* saying. That subtext thing again. The dialog tags melt away as the reader gets emotionally invested in the outcome of the conversation. There's lots of new information too, isn't there? A big giant She's Hiding Something sign is flashing for both Beau and the reader. Are you curious to know what she's hiding? If I did my job right, you should be.

Lining Up Dialog

Conversations are never linear. Avoid the instinct to put your characters through a Q and A session. What I mean by this is having a character ask a question and the other character answer it without evasion or uncertainty.

Here's an example:

"What time are you leaving for the train?" Jamal asked.
"I leave at three," Dana answered.
"Are the Millers meeting you there?"
"Yes. We'll meet and ride the train together."
"What time will you return?"
"The train arrives at one in the afternoon tomorrow," Dana said.
"Do you need me to pick you up?"
"No. I have a ride."

Those kinds of Q and A dialog sessions, while handy for delivering information to your reader, are super boring. No one talks like that. Mix it up.

People don't always speak in full sentences or use correct grammar either. They get interrupted by their own thoughts or by the other person talking over them. Their thoughts might drift off mid-sentence or they won't finish their sentence to build suspense for what they're saying and invite the other person to ask them questions.

Here's an example of dialog from my novel ***Vindicate***:

"I'm taking a really great online class this summer." I never got around to telling him that I quit school last year to work and save money for a possible appeal of his case. Or that the job I took is in a law office, where I have ample access to the law library and case reviews.

"It's not on something stupid like criminal law or how to be a private investigator, is it?"

I shift in my seat.

"Aww, shit, Cora. You promised you'd give up on the stupid idea that you could get me out of here. Why are you wasting your time? I'm a lost cause. Everyone knows it. Take those beauty classes like you always wanted. Face the fact that you can't do what Mom's and Dad's lawyers and the public defender couldn't. I'm done. You're not. You still have a life."

"I don't believe that, Beau, and neither should you. Those charges were bullshit then and they're bullshit now. You didn't kill her. There's no way I'll ever believe it and I'm never going to stop looking for a way to get you out of here."

"Doesn't really matter if I did it or not. I'm convicted, aren't I?"

"I wasn't going to tell you this because I knew what you'd say, but I think I might have a new lead."

He holds up a hand. "Stop it. Stop it, right now."

I ignore him and continue. "I think I found a witness who could—"

"Damn it, Cora! I told you to stop."

Did you notice how the conversation skipped around and how Beau interrupted Cora when she said something he didn't like? This isn't a linear conversation. It twists and turns. At the same time the reader is given information about the characters and their lives. Find a way to feed your reader information without making it *feel* like that's what you're doing.

Exercise:

Next time you're in a restaurant, in line or waiting for the barista to make your latte, listen to the conversations around you. Take note of how people converse. You'll notice that they jump around between topics and that something one of them says can lead to a whole new line of conversation. Use that in your work. Have your character lead—either accidentally or on purpose—the other character into a new subject.

People love to talk about themselves. They listen for opportunities to give the other person information or to get information from them. It's rare for a person to be listening and at the same time not be thinking about what they want to say in return. The next time you're involved in a conversation with someone, pay attention to your own thoughts and desires. What do you hope to get from the interaction with the other person? Did the conversation go the way you wanted it to go or was something left unsaid?

As you can see, dialog is about more than what's being said. It's also a way for you to draw your reader deeper into your story. It's an opportunity to do more, to show more, and to give more to your reader.

Narrowing the Lens

Deep POV is about more than which point of view or views you've chosen to write your novel in. It's the focusing of your novel's camera lens. How wide or tight a shot you want to take will be up to you. In his novel, ***The Art of Fiction***, John Gardner explores what he calls *psychic distance*. Another term you might have heard used which means the same is *narrative distance*. In essence, it's how close the narrative (the reader) stands in relation to your point of view character. The reader could be hovering above your character (the furthest from) or figuratively crawl into and inhabit your character's skin (the closest to).

Using the concept that point of view is a movie camera panning out for wide shots and zooming in for tight shots, let's take a look at how narrative distance can be used to achieve different things at various points in your novel. In ***The Art of Fiction***, Gardner gives an example of a wide shot (example 1), then tightens the shot (examples 2 and 3) until we're as close to the point of view character as we can possibly be (example 4):

> 1) It was winter of the year 1853. A large man stepped out of a doorway.
> 2) Henry J. Warburton had never much cared for snowstorms.
> 3) Henry hated snowstorms.
> 4) Snow. Under your collar, down inside your boots, freezing and plugging up your miserable soul...

I love this example because it succinctly illustrates everything we've been talking about all book long. We go from omniscient point of view (example 1) to deep second person point of view (example 4). Although fiction novels aren't typically written in second person and example 4 feels a little finger-pointy it still makes us feel the cold and misery the character is experiencing. There's also a fair bit of telling going on especially in examples 2 and 3. We're distanced from what the character is thinking and feeling.

Since Gardner's example doesn't quite fit our novel writing needs, let's try it again this time in third person point of view.

> 1) It was winter of the year 1853. A large man stepped out of a doorway.
> 2) Henry J. Warburton had never much

cared for snowstorms.

3) Henry hated snowstorms.

4) Fat chunks of snow filled his collar, his boots, freezing and bitter, making a misery of everything.

Okay, maybe I'm not as poetic as Gardner, but you get the idea. For first person all you'd do is change out *his* collar and *his* boots for *my* collar and *my* boots and you'd still get the same effect.

As you write your novel you'll move the lens in and out, depending on what the scene calls for. For scene transitions—moving the reader from one location to another or moving ahead in time—you'll use a wide shot. For introspection and internal dialog you'll use the tightest shot possible—inhabiting the body of the point of view character. For action scenes and dialog you'll take a mid range shot to capture what the other characters in the story are doing and saying, while maintaining the deepest point of view of your POV character.

If you think of your novel as a movie and deep point of view a camera lens, it might be easier for you to visualize your story as a whole. Be conscious and ever vigilant of where you place your reader in relation to your point of view character. Whenever possible, give the reader the very best angle and tightest shot you can.

In Closing...

I've given you a lot to think about and put into practice. Or at least I hope I have. Don't be lazy in your writing. Give it one hundred percent of your effort one hundred percent of the time. There is no such thing as *good enough* in novel writing. There is only *your very best*. Make sure you're giving your characters and your readers your very best in every sentence, every paragraph, every scene, and every chapter you write.

Never stop learning your craft and stretching your talent as a writer. Attend workshops and online classes. Read as many craft books as you can get your hands on. As you read a novel by another author, pay attention to what other authors are doing and how they do it. What skills do they have that you can apply to your work?

Be bold. Be brave. Be the very best you can be.

And by all means DON'T BE ORDINARY.

Bibliography

Rush by Beth Yarnall
Copyright © 2012 Elizabeth Yarnall

Lush by Beth Yarnall
Copyright © 2014 Elizabeth Yarnall

A Deep and Dark December by Beth Yarnall
Copyright © 2015 Elizabeth Yarnall

Vindicate by Beth Yarnall
Copyright © 2015 Elizabeth Yarnall
Published by Loveswept, an imprint of Random House, a division of Penguin Random House LLC, New York, NY

Atone by Beth Yarnall
Copyright © 2016 Elizabeth Yarnall
Published by Loveswept, an imprint of Random House Publishing Group, a division of Penguin Random House LLC, New York, NY

Reclaim by Beth Yarnall
Copyright © 2016 Elizabeth Yarnall
Published by Loveswept, an imprint of Random House, a division of Penguin Random House LLC, New York, NY

How to Bake a Perfect Life by Barbara O'Neal
Copyright © 2011 Barbara Samuel
Published by Bantam Books, an imprint of Random House Publishing Group, a division of Penguin Random House LLC, New York, NY

Dark Wild Night by Christina Lauren
Copyright © 2015 Christina Hobbs and Lauren Billings
Published by Gallery Books, an imprint of Simon & Schuster, Inc., New York, NY

The Opportunist by Tarryn Fisher
Copyright © 2012 Tarryn Fisher

Rachel's Holiday by Marian Keyes
Copyright © 1998 Marian Keyes
First published in Great Britain by Penguin Books, Ltd.
Hardcover published in 2000 by William Morrow, an imprint of Harper Collins Publishers, LLC

Anybody Out There? by Marian Keyes
Copyright © 2009 Marian Keyes
Published by Harper Collins Publishers, LLC

The Secret Garden by Frances Hodgson Burnette
First published in 1911 and is now public domain

Lord of the Rings by J.R.R. Tolkein
Copyright © 1954, 1965, 1966 by J.R.R. Tolkein
1954 edition copyright renewed 1982 by Christopher R. Tolkein, Michael H. R. Tolkein, John F. R. Tolkein, and Pricilla M. A. R. Tolkein

The Art of Fiction by John Gardner
Copyright © 1983 by the estate of John Gardner
Originally published by Alfred A. Knopf, Inc in 1984

Intimate Behaviour by Desmond Morris
Copyright © 1971 Desmond Morris
Published by Vintage Digital, an imprint of Random House, a division of Penguin Random House LLC, New York, NY

About the Author

Best-selling author, Beth Yarnall, writes mysteries, romantic suspense, and the occasional hilarious tweet. A storyteller since her playground days, Beth remembers her friends asking her to make up stories of how the person 'died' in the slumber party game Light as a Feather, Stiff as a Board, so it's little wonder she prefers writing stories in which people meet unfortunate ends. In middle school she discovered romance novels, which inspired her to write a spoof of soap operas for the school's newspaper. She hasn't stopped writing since.

For a number of years, Beth made her living as a hairstylist and makeup artist and even owned a salon. Somehow hairstylists and salons seem to find their way into her stories. Beth lives in Southern California with her husband, two sons, and their rescue dog where she is hard at work on her next novel.

For more information about Beth and her novels please visit her website:
www.bethyarnall.com

To stay up to date on the latest Beth Yarnall happenings, including new releases, sales, special announcements, exclusive excerpts, and giveaways, subscribe to my newsletter at:
www.bethyarnall.com